THE
DA VINCI CODE
MYSTERIES

THE DA VINCI CODE MYSTERIES

What the Movie Doesn't Tell You

AMY WELBORN

Our Sunday Visitor Publishing Division
Our Sunday Visitor, Inc.
Huntington, Indiana 46750

CONTENTS

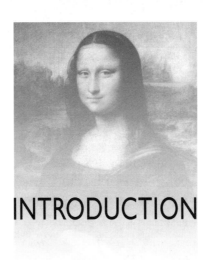

INTRODUCTION

*T*he *Da Vinci Code* is a global phenomenon. The novel by Dan Brown has sold tens of millions of copies, engendered a whole industry of copycats and debunkers, and resulted in the biggest A-listers in Hollywood — including director Ron Howard and actor Tom Hanks — signing up for the movie version. What's not to like?

The answer — for readers and viewers interested in history, religion, and art — is *a lot. The Da Vinci Code* is a mix of fiction and — according to its own first page — fact. It's a thriller that frames a presentation of some intriguing "theories" about Jesus, Mary Magdalene, early Christian history, and art.

This isn't anything new, of course. Historical fiction does this all the time, and there have even been other novels written on the theme of supposed secrets that the Christian Church is determined to suppress. But there's something about *The Da Vinci Code* that's different.

For some reason, a startling number of readers of this novel have embraced the historical theories it presents as authoritative and accurate. As a writer and speaker on *The Da Vinci Code*, I can tell you that this is absolutely true. Declare "It's only a novel" all you want, but the truth is, many readers do believe that they are learning about credible historical hypotheses in this novel.

They're not, of course. None of the assertions in *The Da Vinci Code* — the Jesus-Mary Magdalene connection, the Priory of Sion, the purpose of Leonardo's art — are accepted by academics. This isn't just a matter of religious believers being "afraid of the truth," either, as is sometimes maintained. I guarantee you that if you go to the art history department at the most secular university in the world and declare that John in *The Last Supper* is really Mary Magdalene, and that Leonardo did this because he wanted to communicate the truth about the Holy Grail, the professors will laugh at you. They will. Are they part of the conspiracy of fearful Christians, too? Not quite.

This book answers some of the most frequently asked questions about the historical assertions in *The Da Vinci Code*. More detail is available in my other books *de-coding Da Vinci: The Facts Behind the Fiction of 'The Da Vinci Code'* and *de-coding Mary Magdalene: Truth, Legend, and Lies*. This book also focuses on material that made it from the novel to the screen version, so if you want more information on issues that were dropped from the movie version, go to these other books for more.

It's my hope that this little book will clear up some confusion. I hope that it will encourage readers and viewers of the movie, if they are interested in Jesus and early Christianity, to learn more by studying reliable works on the subject, rather than the mostly fictional, pseudo-history that Dan Brown used in writing his novel.

I also hope, more than anything else, that those readers and viewers who are interested in novels that grapple with issues of faith and spirituality will be inspired to go beyond *The Da Vinci Code* — far beyond it — and try some of the titles I suggest in the Epilogue, books by writers who take faith seriously and grapple with it with skill, artistry, and the thoughtfulness that this most important part of life deserves.

one

BACK TO THE SOURCES

1. *The Da Vinci Code* is a novel. Don't you understand that?

Yes, we do. But amazingly, and perhaps unfortunately, millions of readers of *The Da Vinci Code* have come to believe, for whatever reason, that the assertions that this work makes about history reflect the real work and opinions of serious academic scholars. They don't.

2. What are those assertions?

The most important ones, and those that found their way from the novel to the movie, are:

- What Christianity says about Jesus is wrong.
- The real story about Jesus is to be found in Gnostic writings from the third, fourth, and fifth centuries.
- Emperor Constantine repressed writings that reflected the real Jesus and commissioned new writings.
- Jesus was married to Mary Magdalene.
- Their union produced a child.
- Mary Magdalene was the real "Holy Grail," as the one "holding" the blood of Jesus in the form of his child.
- This secret has been protected by a group called the Priory of Sion.
- Leonardo da Vinci was a member of the Priory of Sion and hid the secret in codes in his artwork.
- Opus Dei is a "radical sect" dedicated to opposing this secret.

3.   Where did these ideas come from?

They came from a number of different sources, most of which are actually cited by Dan Brown in his book or on his website. None of these sources are considered credible by academic historians.

4.   What are these sources?

The sources most important to *The Da Vinci Code* are:

- *Holy Blood, Holy Grail*, written by Michael Baigent, who has a degree in psychology, Richard Leigh, a novelist, and Henry Lincoln, a television actor and producer. Most of the foundational ideas — including the notion of the Priory of Sion protecting the bloodline of Jesus and Mary Magdalene, which is violently opposed by the Catholic Church — come from this book.
- *The Templar Revelation: Secret Guardians of the True Identity of Christ*, by Lynn Picknett and Clive Prince, who also co-authored *Stargate Conspiracy: The Truth about Extraterrestrial Life and the Mysteries of Ancient Egypt*. This book provided Brown with the Leonardo da Vinci angle.
- *The Woman with the Alabaster Jar: Mary Magdalen and the Holy Grail*, by Margaret Starbird. Starbird has written many books on the marriage of Jesus and Mary Magdalene and on her status as a near-goddess, as well as on the identity of their child, whom she calls Sarah.

5.   How does Dan Brown use these sources?

If you've read *The Da Vinci Code*, you know that the novel consists of a rather spare plot involving lots of chases and cliff-hangers, framed around long conversations in which characters explain things to one another. The historical assertions are contained in these speeches.

6.   Has there been any reaction to Brown's use of these sources?

Two of the authors of *Holy Blood, Holy Grail* — Baigent and Leigh — have filed suit against Random House, the publisher of *The*

Da Vinci Code, in British courts, claiming infringement on their ideas — a form of plagiarism.

In addition, American novelist Lewis Perdue has sued Brown and Random House, claiming that Brown's novel plagiarizes his own book, a novel entitled *Daughter of God*, published in 2001.

7.   What's wrong with using these sources as the basis of a novel?

Nothing. Writers can create their works in any way they choose. We have no opinion on whether Brown's use of the works he cites constitutes unfair use or plagiarism. He does, after all, cite them.

(However, it must be said that *if* the authors of *Holy Blood, Holy Grail* actually believed that what they were presenting was simply historical fact, they would have no grounds to sue for plagiarism. If I write a book about Abraham Lincoln, and you follow up with your own biography, I can't sue you for saying that Lincoln was assassinated by John Wilkes Booth. It's only if those authors know that what they wrote was fictional, and their own creation, that they actually would have a case for plagiarism.)

However, the problem, as we'll see in the course of this short book, is that Brown leaves the reader with the clear impression that these sources are reliable, sound historical works. They're not. There is a great deal of scholarship on the history of early Christianity, and of course, not all scholars share identical interpretations of the period. But even among the diverse scholarly views on Jesus, on early Christianity and the identities of Mary Magdalene, and on the Holy Grail — not to mention the role of Leonardo da Vinci and some purported "Priory of Sion" in all of this — *the theories proposed in* The Da Vinci Code *play no role.*

This is so important to understand. You can pick almost any historian of early Christianity who is a non-Christian and skeptical of the Christian story of Jesus and ask, "So, was Jesus' message really about the union of the masculine and feminine principles, and did he really pick Mary Magdalene to bear this message, and was she the real

Holy Grail?" and I can almost promise you that the historian would laugh.

8.   What did Dan Brown leave out?

This is really the most important question. If you're trying to unpack the mysteries of Jesus and early Christianity, you would probably want to use what are considered to be the most reliable sources around. If you were *really* interested in presenting the whole story and exploring possibilities that are related to what scholars think might have actually happened, you would do that. And what would those sources be?

Believe it or not, it would be the writings that the earliest Christians themselves produced.

Imagine that.

But Brown doesn't do that. All of the New Testament writings were composed before the end of the first century. There is a wealth of other early Christian writings, including sermons, teachings, and even prayers from those early years. They say many interesting things, but Brown ignores them completely.

9.   Why?

Once you start reading these early Christian writings, the answer becomes pretty clear. *The Da Vinci Code* is about a mystery. It's about secrets, supposedly hidden for hundreds of years, secrets that would just blow everything we thought we knew to pieces. That's what the movie trailer says, isn't it?

"Right before our eyes . . . a secret that could change the course of mankind . . . forever."

The problem is, once you start looking beyond *The Da Vinci Code* at the most trustworthy sources available, you find something interesting:

- The secrets and mysteries in *The Da Vinci Code* . . . aren't.
- The real history of early Christianity certainly holds questions, but the central mission of Jesus is no mystery.

And *this* is what is so important to remember about *The Da Vinci Code* and its "mysteries": What's mysterious isn't what's in there — it's what's *left out*.

FOR MORE INFORMATION ...

For more information about the sources used in The Da Vinci Code, *see the Introduction and Chapter One of* de-coding Da Vinci: The Facts Behind the Fiction of 'The Da Vinci Code' *(Our Sunday Visitor).*

two

THE PRIORY OF SION

10. What does *The Da Vinci Code* say about the Priory of Sion?

In both the novel and the movie, the Priory of Sion is the keeper of the secret of the "real" Jesus, and the protector of the bloodline of Jesus and Mary Magdalene.

The book contains a frontpiece entitled "Fact," in which Dan Brown lists the Priory of Sion as a "real organization" founded in 1099. He says that in 1975, documents listing the leadership of this group were discovered in the Bibliothèque Nationale (French National Library).

The novel goes into further detail, as does the movie. As recounted in *The Da Vinci Code*, the Priory of Sion is a secret society, founded in 1099 by Godfrey de Bouillon. The group, with its military arm, the Knights Templar, was founded to guard a secret hidden and recovered in Jerusalem.

That secret, of course, concerns Mary Magdalene's identity as Jesus' companion, mother of his child, source of some sort of "sacred feminine" principle, and matriarch of the Merovingian royal line.

11. Simple question: Is this true?

Simple answer: No.

All of this Priory of Sion business reflects the oddities of what's known as "esoteric history," its close cousin, "conspiracy theories," and its grandfather, "fraud."

12. What's the story?

There's a lot, as there always is when you start delving into so-called secret societies. It can get very convoluted and complex. But really, when it comes to the Priory of Sion, what you need to know is basically this: Yes, there was a French group called the Priory of Sion. It was formally registered with the French government in 1956.

The trouble is, that was the first time it was registered, and its purpose had nothing to do with Grails or bloodlines at that time.

13. So what was it?

The main force behind the Priory of Sion — which never got more than a few members — was Pierre Plantard. A truly shady character whose life was one long series of schemes and delusions, Plantard was born in 1920, and he spent most of the 1930s and 1940s creating phantom associations dedicated to his pet causes: restoration of the French monarchy, sympathy with the Vichy regime, and anti-Semitism. He spent some time in prison for failing to register one of these associations, as well as for fraud.

He was working as a draftsman when he and his friends formed the Priory of Sion, also known by the acronym CIRCUIT (translated from the French as Chivalry of Catholic Rule and Institution and of Independent Traditionalist Union).

The group worked on two levels. Practically, it was dedicated to affirming the right to low-cost housing for locals. But on a more exalted level, the group was a typical esoteric pseudo-Masonic society, with degrees of membership and secret initiations.

14. Why was it named "Priory of Sion"?

It was named, not to recall "Zion" or Jerusalem, but after a mountain near Plantard's village — Mount Sion, of course.

15. Where does the bloodline business come in?

After some jail time, perhaps related to suspicious activity with a minor, Plantard moved to Paris, where he made a living as a psychic.

He came across a story from the previous century about a priest in a small parish in Rennes-le-Chateau who obtained an apparently inexplicable fortune. The priest claimed it was because he had found a treasure, which could have been material treasure, or perhaps secrets that brought him into circles of French power. No one was really sure. The priest's name was Sauniere.

16. Sauniere? Isn't that the name of the murdered curator in The Da Vinci Code?

Yes, it is. Some have wondered at Brown's choice, which indicates that he knows of this story — the real story of the Priory of Sion — which, in turn, calls into question his assertion that the account giving the group more ancient roots is "fact," as the first page of his novel suggests.

17. What did Plantard do with this story?

Working with a Philippe de Chérisey, Plantard created a new backstory for the Priory of Sion: that it was a group, originating during the time of the Crusades, dedicated to protecting the secret found at Rennes-le-Chateau. What was the secret? It was that the Merovingian line was the true royal family of France, not the Carolingians or the Bourbons. The Priory of Sion was the protector of this secret.

With an associate, Plantard created false documents supporting this, including a list of "Grand Masters" of the Priory of Sion, a list that naturally included Leonardo da Vinci. Between 1965 and 1967, Plantard and a friend deposited these documents in the French National Library, where they were "discovered" by another accomplice, Gérard de Sède, who wrote a book about the purported secret in 1967, *L'Or de Rennes* ("The Gold of Rennes").

18. How was the truth revealed?

During the 1980s, de Chérisey revealed the truth, and the fraud was widely exposed in the French media.

19. There's nothing about Jesus or Mary Magdalene in this story. Why?

That element was added by Henry Lincoln, actor and television producer, who discovered Plantard's story and embellished it with the "Jesus-Mary Magdalene as Grail" element, which became the basis of *Holy Blood, Holy Grail.*

20. What happened to Plantard?

He died in 2000, but not until trying to resuscitate the Priory of Sion one more time, this time in a more general, New-Age kind of form, focused on the energy emanating from a mountain near Rennes-le-Chateau.

21. How did that priest Sauniere get rich, anyway?

In an investigation, his bishop discovered that Sauniere had been soliciting Mass stipends from all over Europe, to the point where he was gathering stipends for five thousand to six thousand Masses every year.

From beginning to end, the story of the Priory of Sion is one of deceit, fraud, and fantasy. For reasonable people, that should close the book on the purported "history" contained in *The Da Vinci Code* once and for all.

22. Where can I find more information?

Priory of Sion central on the Internet is this site, run by Paul Smith: http://priory-of-sion.com. It contains detailed timelines and copies of many relevant documents.

three

OPUS DEI

23. What role does Opus Dei play in *The Da Vinci Code*?

Not a good one. In *The Da Vinci Code*, two major characters are members of Opus Dei: Bishop Aringarosa, the head of the organization, and Silas, the notorious albino Opus Dei monk.

As backstory to the plot, a new pope has made it clear he would like to dismantle Opus Dei. Bishop Aringarosa, seeking to preserve the group, accepts the offer of a mysterious "Teacher" to give the bishop information that the Church would presumably prefer to keep secret. In this way, the bishop can essentially blackmail the Church into letting Opus Dei continue to exist.

24. What is the "secret" that the Church wishes to keep?

The secret, of course, concerns Jesus, Mary Magdalene, and the Grail, and it has been protected by the Priory of Sion. The Teacher wants the Grand Masters of the Priory of Sion killed (because, it is later revealed, the Teacher is actually the scholar Teabing, who wants to reveal the information that the Priory has decided to keep secret). The bishop enlists his protégé, Silas, who does the dirty work.

25. So? What's wrong with this? Isn't it just a story?

Yes, *The Da Vinci Code* is fiction. But in this case, it uses an organization that really exists as an element in the plot, and it ends up mischaracterizing and — we'll go so far to say — defaming and libeling it.

26. What! No albino monks in Opus Dei?

No monks at all, as a matter of fact. Let's begin at the beginning.

The Da Vinci Code leaves one with the distinct impression that Opus Dei is a cult that seeks to obtain and keep power in the Catholic Church. It is referred to as a "radical fundamentalist" "sect" that considers its members the only true Christians. This is simply not true.

27. What is Opus Dei?

Opus Dei is a Latin phrase that means "Work of God." It was established in Spain in 1928 by a priest named Josemaría Escrivá. Escrivá (who was canonized as a saint in 2002) wanted to help laypeople really live their faith in the world. He wanted all people to understand that whatever they were doing in the world could be the "Work of God" if they approached it that way. The focus of Opus Dei is on helping ordinary Christians follow Christ more closely in the midst of their lives in the world.

28. How many members does it have? Who are they?

There are about 85,000 Opus Dei members worldwide. About 2 percent of them are priests, and the rest are laypeople. The membership of Opus Dei is divided almost equally between men and women. There are about 30,000 Opus Dei members in the United States.

There are different levels of membership. *Supernumeraries* make up about 70 percent of the membership of Opus Dei. These are people who commit to the spiritual formation and discipline offered by Opus Dei, and who live in the world — married, if that is their vocation.

Numeraries are committed to celibacy. They live in Opus Dei centers. Some work in the world, others devote themselves to apostolates sponsored by Opus Dei — education, health care, and spiritual formation are the most common.

Opus Dei priests are members of the Priestly Society of the Holy Cross. Some priests associated with the Society are full members of this prelature, and others are diocesan priests who stay associated with their diocese, under the authority of their bishop, but who have found the spiritual formation provided by Opus Dei helpful in their spiritual lives and ministries.

So, yes, membership includes laypeople from all over the world, as well as priests and even bishops. But there are absolutely no monks. Monks are members of monastic religious orders like the Benedictines or Cistercians. Opus Dei is not a religious order.

29. So what *is* it?

You're confused. That's not surprising, because *The Da Vinci Code* is confused as well, referring, at different times, to the group as a "sect," a "Vatican prelature," a "congregation," and even "a Catholic Church." Brown does get it right, though, when he says that Opus Dei is a "personal prelature," even though he gets the definition of that term incorrect. He implies that this means that the group exists at the service of a *person*, the pope, as if it's his personal "Enforcers of the Faith," which is not what it means at all.

The two major types of organizing principles of groups within the Church are dioceses and religious orders. A diocese is a geographical territory, with the entire world divided up into Catholic dioceses. The bishop of a diocese — along with the parishes within that diocese — has a responsibility to serve the spiritual and corporal needs of the Catholics of that diocese. It is territorial.

Religious orders are not geographically confined (although a religious order must get permission from a bishop in order to start its ministry in a particular diocese). They are made up of individuals who take vows — usually of chastity, poverty, and obedience — and who minister according to a particular charism. So some religious orders are dedicated to education, health care, or even contemplative prayer.

You can see that Opus Dei really doesn't fit into either of these categories. It is international in scope, so it is not territorial. It is primarily made up of laypeople, who may commit to the spiritual formation offered by Opus Dei, but not take vows in the same sense that members of religious orders do.

In order to find a way to fit Opus Dei into the administrative structure of the Church, in the early 1960s the idea of a "personal prelature" was suggested and ultimately approved. Opus Dei is structured so that the prelate — the head — has authority, not over territory (which is normal), but over the persons in the association.

30. Give me some examples of the work of Opus Dei.

The primary work of Opus Dei is in personal spiritual formation. Individuals who become part of Opus Dei follow a particular spiritual path of prayer, charitable works, and moral life that they have chosen because they find it helpful. *The Da Vinci Code* accuses Opus Dei of arrogance, of declaring that its way is the only true way, but that is simply not the case. The spiritual path laid out by St. Escrivá and Opus Dei is helpful to some, and not to others.

Aside from the spiritual work, many members of Opus Dei engage in educational and health care work, as well as ministry to the poor. These schools, hospitals, and other institutions are not actually owned by the Prelature of Opus Dei itself, but by those who institute them.

31. But I've heard that Opus Dei wields a lot of power in the Catholic Church. Is this true?

No. According to journalist John Allen, whose book *Opus Dei: Secrets and Power Inside the Catholic Church* is a well-researched and objective look at the group, out of 4,564 bishops in the world, 39 are members of Opus Dei — .8 percent. Out of 2,500 workers in the Roman Curia — the central administrative offices of the Church in Vatican City — 20 are members of Opus Dei, and of those only 3 are in head offices, and only 1 in an office that makes any kind of policy.

32. What about that wire that Silas puts around his leg? What about his self-flagellation? Isn't that a part of Opus Dei?

There's certainly some truth there. But it's a truth that has to be seen in context.

Sacrifice is an important element in the Christian faith. We understand that Jesus' love for the world was expressed most deeply in his sacrificial death on the cross. We understand that real love involves sacrifice.

In addition, growth in holiness requires sacrifices of all kinds. Why? Because "holiness" is really another word for the love of God and our neighbor. No one grows in love by being selfish. No one grows spiritually by pursuing whatever pleasures appeal to him or her at the moment. This is nothing unique to Christianity. If you read any of the world's great spiritual teachers, they will tell you exactly the same thing: Sacrifice is an essential part of the spiritual life.

Opus Dei members keep this truth in mind as they go about their daily lives. They are, as are all Christians, encouraged to sacrifice momentary pleasures and desires for the sake of love.

In addition, some use methods of what we call "corporal mortification" as a way to help them grow in holiness. This is done only if a spiritual director agrees that it might be helpful.

The *cilice* — a chain that is worn around one's leg — as well as a "discipline" — a small stick with cords attached — have long histories in Christian spirituality. Their use is ultimately rooted in Jesus' words in Luke 9:23, when he reminds his disciples that part of following him involves taking up a cross.

Using these means of corporal mortification is intended to help individuals free themselves from attachment to physical pleasure. It does not imply hatred of the body, but rather a recognition of what the ultimate purpose of the body is: like the soul, to serve God and his children. In denying ourselves — the thinking goes — we will be strengthened when the moment comes in which we are called to sacrifice for the sake of love.

As we noted before, corporal mortification is found in most world religions, often in the form of extreme fasting or even difficult and challenging prayer positions.

Additionally, it might help to remember that modern people actually do understand the concept of "No pain, no gain" very well.

We are willing to go to heroic lengths, and cause ourselves much suffering — enduring hunger pains and workout burn — in order to get the body we want. Similarly, since ancient times, human beings have recognized that physical sacrifice might play a part in getting the soul we want.

33. So what's the final word on Opus Dei and *The Da Vinci Code?*

It should be clear that Opus Dei — a group of devout, hardworking Christians — has been incredibly maligned by its portrayal in *The Da Vinci Code.* It is puzzling as to why Dan Brown and the producers of the movie, given the option of inventing a fictitious group to serve the story's purposes, would select a real organization, and then slander it, without apology.

FOR MORE INFORMATION . . .

See the Opus Dei website at http://www. opusdei.org *and the book* Opus Dei: Secrets and Power Inside the Catholic Church, *by John Allen (Penguin).*

four

EARLY CHRISTIAN HISTORY

34. Christianity started a long time ago. It must be hard to figure out who Jesus was and what he said and did.

Yes, Christianity did begin almost two thousand years ago. But surprisingly, there are quite a few surviving texts that help us get a good idea of what early Christianity was like.

Of course, there are huge gaps and big questions, and not a little ambiguity. That's what keeps historians in business. However, when you consider that we're talking about a relatively tiny religious movement that started in the backwaters of the Roman Empire, was primarily located in people's homes, and whose founder was executed as a criminal, it's surprising what has survived from the first century: the Gospels, homilies and letters from bishops and other teachers, moral and theological instruction, prayers, and even some liturgical and artistic evidence.

35. Yes, I know. Dan Brown uses a lot of this to explain the history of Christianity in *The Da Vinci Code*.

Actually, he doesn't. It's one of the more important things to realize if you're making the mistake of looking to this novel or movie as a source of reliable historical information. There are literally volumes of texts surviving from this period. Brown cites none of them, including, most tellingly, the works written closest to the lifetime of Jesus himself.

36. What are those texts?

The letters of Paul and the Gospels that are found in the New Testament. Scholars believe, for example, that the first book of what we now call the New Testament — Paul's first letter to the Thessalonians — was written around the years A.D. 57-58, a little more than twenty years after Jesus' death.

37. But wait. *The Da Vinci Code* does mention gospels — the "Gnostic Gospels." Those are real, right?

Yes, indeed, there are writings that are today called the Gnostic Gospels. But they don't tell us anything useful about the earliest days of Christianity, or about Jesus' ministry, or even about Mary Magdalene.

38. How do you know?

Because the books that *The Da Vinci Code* cites as evidence are dated much later than the New Testament writings. They date from the late second century, at the very earliest, to the early fifth century.

39. I find that hard to believe. We're talking about texts that were written two thousand years ago. I don't believe that there's any way to tell what texts accurately reflect what really happened and what's made up in such old documents. I think you just have to pick one and go with it.

Historians would disagree — and vehemently. Dating of ancient texts does involve judgment calls and is always disputable, but in general there is little or no disagreement that the Gnostic writings Brown uses tell us nothing historical about the ministry of Jesus. They're about something else.

40. What are they about?

Well, they're about Gnosticism. They're about a Gnostic interpretation of Jesus and his ministry.

41. What's Gnosticism?

Gnosticism was a spiritual movement in the ancient Near East and Roman Empire, which flourished from the first through the fifth centuries. Gnosticism wasn't organized, and Gnostic ideas touched many religious traditions, including Judaism and Christianity.

Gnostic belief was diverse, but most of the time it hinged on a couple of common points: that the material world was evil and was created by an evil being, and that the spiritual world was good and was created by a good deity.

The point of life was to free the imprisoned spiritual spark from within your evil body so that it could attain eternal life. This was done through rituals and the learning of passwords that would get you through various levels in the afterlife.

As we said, there is much more to Gnosticism than that — and it was a diverse movement — but that's enough to get us started.

42. What were the Gnostic Gospels, then?

What some call the "Gnostic Gospels" are simply Gnostic interpretations of Jesus. These writings are completely different from the New Testament Gospels in both content and tone. They are clearly coming from a different time and place, not to mention a different theological perspective.

43. How are they different?

The New Testament Gospels:

- Are composed of many stories relating to Jesus' ministry: healings, parables, preaching, encounters with people. They are varied and specific in detail.
- Contain accounts of his birth to a human mother and of his suffering and death.
- Have the feel of real life about them — people are flawed, make mistakes, regret their actions.
- Agree on the essence of Jesus' ministry: preaching the kingdom of God; being in conflict with Jewish religious authority; scan-

dalizing onlookers because of his attitude toward the Law, as well as his teaching that he would be put to death and then rise from the dead.

The Gnostic writings:

- Are almost all dialogues between Jesus and one or more of the apostles. These dialogues are lengthy and abstract.
- Do not include any material about Jesus' birth, suffering, or death, because Gnostics believed that the body was evil, and that human material existence could not be anything good or holy.
- Read like speeches composed to support a predetermined philosophy.
- Contain a radically different theology than what we read in the New Testament Gospels.

44. Well, I like the Gnostic Gospels better. I pick them.

Go ahead. But know that your choice makes no sense, intellectually speaking. If you're interested in the truth about Jesus' life and ministry, you will, like every serious scholar out there, begin with the writings in the New Testament.

45. But the Gnostic Gospels *could be* accurate. Anything's possible, right?

No, it's not. Jesus was a real person who said and did specific things. Although in the centuries since, people have disagreed vehemently on the meaning of those words and actions, and even though one's final decision about who Jesus was is a matter of faith, the fact is that the early witnesses are consistent in their account of Jesus' emphasis in his preaching, and in the general outline of his life. The Gnostic interpretation, coming centuries later, is different — and it is rooted, not in historical events, but in Gnostic ideas.

FOR MORE INFORMATION . . .

To find out more about the Gnostic writings, see Chapter One of de-coding Da Vinci: The Facts Behind the Fiction of 'The Da Vinci Code' *(Our Sunday Visitor).*

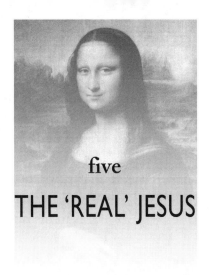

five

THE 'REAL' JESUS

46. What does *The Da Vinci Code* say about Jesus?

Both the novel and the movie maintain that Jesus was a purely mortal teacher of divine wisdom. They claim that the focus of his message, besides love, was the reunion of the masculine and the feminine principles of reality. He embodied this teaching in his life via his marriage to Mary Magdalene, whom he selected to carry on his message.

There is the claim that Christians didn't believe that Jesus was divine until they were forced into it by Emperor Constantine in 325.

47. What's wrong with this?

There's no evidence to support it. The best evidence we have says consistently that Jesus preached and taught within the context of first-century Judaism, using Jewish concepts and images. He didn't speak of masculine and feminine forces within reality. He didn't even speak just vague words about love. He spoke about the kingdom of God, about turning from sin, about depending on God, and about loving one's neighbor.

And the material concerning Constantine is just completely off, as even a brief look at a secular textbook could tell you.

48. So where does this vision of Jesus in *The Da Vinci Code* come from?

It comes, first of all, from modern writings like Margaret Starbird's *The Woman with the Alabaster Jar*. In turn, these writers draw on their interpretations of some Gnostic writings.

49. *The Da Vinci Code* **says that its version is the "real" Jesus, and that the Gospels in the New Testament were created so that the truth could be suppressed.**

This, of course, is just silly. The core of Christian belief about Jesus' identity and mission was consistently articulated from the time of the earliest writings about Jesus, which, by their own admission, are based on the recollections of witnesses to his life. Paul, for example, was taught by and knew some of Jesus' apostles, and he was a part of the Christian communities that had been taught and formed by them. His writings reflect a clear belief that Jesus was the Son of God, and those writings date from the mid-first century.

50. **Dan Brown seems to claim that this was all politics, that this story — Peter's side — was picked because the story of Mary Magdalene's leadership was too radical. Peter's party wanted power.**

Again, this makes no sense, and there is no evidence to support it. The process of selecting books for the canon of Scripture is no mystery — and, by the way, most of it had happened long before Constantine came onto the scene.

By the early second century, the Christian writers whose works have survived consistently cite Matthew, Mark, Luke, and John as the most authoritative accounts of Jesus' ministry. Why? Because they "repress" the story of Mary Magdalene?

No, because — and this is what *they say themselves* — these are the accounts that have the closest ties to the apostles, and are closest in content to what the apostles taught about Jesus. In short, they reflect what happened. *That's* why they were seen as the most authoritative. That's what *authoritative* means.

The "power theory" is also illogical for this simple reason: If the "Peter party" that "selected the Gospels" did so in order to malign Mary Magdalene, then they did a terrible job, considering that the whole Resurrection account hinges on her witness and testimony.

51. What about Constantine?

The Da Vinci Code makes two main claims about Constantine:

1. That he was responsible for selecting the four canonical Gospels and discarding the rest. (We've already seen how that's not true.)
2. That until Constantine's reign, Christians didn't believe in the divinity of Jesus, and that he forced that belief upon Christianity as a way of supporting his own reign as sole ruler of the empire.

This second claim is as absurd as the first. The proceedings of the Council of Nicaea, the time during which all of this supposedly happened, were summarized at the time, and they are not secret. The Bible was not their focus — for the books of the canon had been largely established by then.

No, the focus of this council was Jesus' identity. There was a heresy called Arianism that was growing in popularity. Arius' heresy taught that Jesus wasn't fully divine, and instead that he was some sort of semi-divine son of God. This heresy was dividing the Church, so Constantine called the council so that the bishops could deal with it. Their response was to carefully define, to the extent possible, what it means to say that Jesus is both fully human and fully divine. The fruits of their labors are in the Nicene Creed.

Finally, the whole "Constantine forcing Jesus' divinity" scenario makes no sense because we have almost three hundred years of texts preceding the Council of Nicaea that very vividly show what early Christians thought of Jesus. They worshiped him as Lord, and they believed that through his death and resurrection they were saved from sin.

The "sacred feminine" is, unsurprisingly, not mentioned.

52. *The Da Vinci Code* says that the divinity of Jesus was voted on by this council. That's a strange way to come up with a doctrine. That would seem to prove the point that it was all politics.

Not at all. First of all, the "vote" that was taken at the council was not about Jesus' divinity, but about the condemnation of Arius' ideas, and a positive assertion about what the apostolic witness to Jesus meant. The vote was on the content of what we now call the Nicene Creed, on whether this was an accurate sense of the faith witnessed to by the apostles and preserved in the Gospels and in Tradition: 316 bishops voted "yes" and 2 voted "no." The vote wasn't even close, and it wasn't a vote on Jesus' divinity, which all Christians had believed for centuries, anyway.

53. But don't those Gnostic writings reflect another view of Jesus that could be equally legitimate?

Well, those writings do reflect something: namely, the views of Gnostic heretics, who reshaped the story of Jesus that was handed down by the apostles to fit their own philosophy. But their writings have no relationship to what Jesus actually said and did in the first century.

54. What else is wrong with the picture of Jesus in *The Da Vinci Code?*

A lot, of course, but one of the more interesting points to note is how in *The Da Vinci Code* Jesus is completely taken out of his Jewish context. Sure, his marriage to Mary Magdalene is presented as the union of two Jewish royal bloodlines, but that's it.

Jesus was a first-century Jewish teacher. He taught in synagogues, worshiped in synagogues, and his message, as presented in the Gospels, makes the most sense when you understand the context — the whole history of God's relationship with Israel, as related in the Old Testament, or Hebrew Scriptures.

It's a rather interesting question. Why does Dan Brown strip Jesus of his Jewish theological, spiritual, and historical context? What possible purpose could that serve?

There's also a fundamental illogic at the heart of this. *The Da Vinci Code* is all about "proving" that Jesus is "only" human and not at all divine. But then we're asked to believe that Mary Magdalene is some sort of divine presence and goddess. At the end of the movie, we're presented with a scene that suggests that Sophie, as the descendent of Jesus, has some sort of divine power. If any of this makes sense to you, congratulations. Or, our condolences. Whichever you prefer!

FOR MORE INFORMATION...

To find out more about Jesus' life and ministry, see Chapters Three and Four of decoding Da Vinci: The Facts Behind the Fiction of 'The Da Vinci Code' (Our Sunday Visitor).

six

MARY MAGDALENE

55. What does *The Da Vinci Code* say about Mary Magdalene?

A lot — some of it contradictory and most of it fantasy.

According to *The Da Vinci Code*, Mary Magdalene was a woman of royal blood who was a disciple of Jesus, who was his wife or lover, and who bore his child.

She was the disciple Jesus wanted to lead his movement.

She was the real "Holy Grail."

She was the embodiment of the ideal of the "sacred feminine" and, in fact, a sort of goddess herself.

Her image and influence have been demeaned, demonized, and repressed by the Catholic Church for two thousand years, as she's been identified as a whore.

56. That's impressive. She was evidently quite something. Is all of this true?

One thing: Mary Magdalene was, indeed, a disciple — a follower — of Jesus. No doubt about that.

57. But nothing else? How do you know?

The same way we know about anything else in the past — the evidence doesn't support it.

58. *The Da Vinci Code* **uses evidence, evidence that proves all of these points about Mary Magdalene.**

We've already covered the weakness of the "evidence" used in *The Da Vinci Code*. The same applies to what that "evidence" says about Mary Magdalene. We'll take the points one by one. But first, we'll briefly list what we do know about Mary Magdalene:

- Mary Magdalene is mentioned several times in the Gospels. She is first introduced by Luke (8:1-3), in which she is described as one of a group of women who accompanied Jesus and the apostles, "who provided for them out of their means." She is described specifically as a woman from whom Jesus drove out seven demons.
- She is not mentioned again until the end of the Gospels. She is consistently described as being present at the cross, along with other women, including Mary, Jesus' mother (Matthew 27:55-56; Mark 15:40-41; Luke 23:49 [as one of the women "from Galilee"]; John 19:25).
- In every Gospel, Mary Magdalene is among the first witnesses of the empty tomb and the Risen Christ: (Matthew 28:1-10; Mark 16:1-11; Luke 24:1-11; John 20:1-18).

That's it. That is all we can discern from the Gospels, which, you might want to remember, were all written within a few decades after the events they describe.

59. So what does that tell us about Mary Magdalene?

It tells us that she was an important figure in early Christianity, a woman who was so grateful for what Jesus had done for her that she left everything to follow him. She was faithful and courageous as well.

60. But *The Da Vinci Code* **says that she was also Jesus' wife. Teabing, the scholar character, even says that the idea is widely accepted among historians.**

It's not. There are no serious historians of early Christianity who believe that Jesus and Mary Magdalene were married.

61. Maybe it wasn't mentioned because it was scandalous, or because the other early Christians didn't want it known.

This is a rather common hypothesis, but it fails on a number of levels:

- The Gospels are all very forthright about naming Jesus' relatives and even comment on his sometimes-rocky relationship with them. If he had a wife, there would be no reason not to mention her as well.
- There would have been no "scandal" in Jesus being a married man. While there was definitely a tradition in Judaism of prophets being unmarried, being married was normal. Again, Jews of the first century would have had no reason to hide this.

62. So where does the idea come from?

Two places. First, it comes from those books of pseudo-history that we mentioned in the first chapter. They all suggest some kind of relationship between Jesus and Mary Magdalene.

Second, in the Gnostic writings we discussed in the fourth chapter, Mary Magdalene is described, in a couple of points, as being a "companion" of Jesus, and as being kissed by him "on the mouth." Some modern interpreters take this to mean a sexual relationship.

63. How could it mean anything else?

Easily:

- Remember, the Gnostic writings do not, it is generally agreed, reflect the events of the first century, but rather interpretations of those events from a Gnostic perspective, centuries later.
- For that reason, the role that individual characters play in these writings should be seen in symbolic rather than historical terms. So the prominence of Mary Magdalene reflects the emphasis in some (but by no means all) Gnostic systems on gender as a metaphor for spiritual reality. It might also reflect the Gnostic hostility to orthodox Christianity, which traces its authority to Peter and the Twelve.

- To get even more specific, the passages cited by *The Da Vinci Code* are not nearly as unambiguous as Brown would have you believe. The Greek word we translate as "companion" in this text is never used as a synonym for "wife" in other Greek texts.
- The "kissing text," from the Gnostic *Gospel of Philip*, is unclear. The text is damaged, and it doesn't actually say "on the mouth." In addition, in Gnostic texts, such an action would be symbolic — of Jesus sharing his wisdom with Mary.

64. Well, then, that leads to the next issue. So they weren't married. These texts indicate that she was a privileged disciple, and that the other apostles, mainly Peter, were jealous of her.

That's right. And in another Gnostic work, the *Pistis Sophia*, the apostles are described as being jealous of Mary, the mother of Jesus. It's odd that modern interpreters ignore that point.

As we've said before, these Gnostic writings do not reflect first-century history, but rather the concerns and interpretation of third-, fourth-, and fifth-century Gnostics.

65. What about the Holy Grail?

There has been enormous scholarly work done on the history and mythology of the Holy Grail. None of the hundreds of years of Grail lore indicate that anyone, anywhere, associated it with Mary Magdalene. That's a twentieth-century invention.

66. But surely Mary Magdalene's image has suffered in Christianity. That's what *The Da Vinci Code* says.

Once again, cold hard logic is quite useful here:

- If "Peter's party" composed and selected the texts we have in the New Testament today, and if they wanted to demonize Mary Magdalene through that process, they did a rotten job. If this was their agenda, why did they leave Mary Magdalene at the center of the central Christian story — the resurrection of Jesus?

- Mary Magdalene is honored *as a saint* by the Catholic Church. By the fifth century, she was frequently depicted in art, mentioned in sermons, and had hymns written in her honor. By the eighth century, her feast day had been established: July 22, which is the same date the Church celebrates her today.
- She was, after the Blessed Virgin Mary, the most popular saint of the Middle Ages. Churches were named after her, her shrines were popular pilgrimage sites, she was a popular character in medieval mystery plays, and she was a fixture in art.

That's an odd way to demonize a person.

67. However, she *was* labeled as a "prostitute," and the Scriptures don't say that she was any such thing. That sounds like demonizing to me.

It wasn't. Mary Magdalene came to be identified as a prostitute, or at least as a woman whose previous sins were sexual, when some writers, confused by the number of Marys and unnamed sinful women in the Gospels, began to wonder if they all weren't one and the same person.

In 591, Pope Gregory the Great preached a homily in which he brought these questions to the surface, and he ended up conflating various New Testament figures: Mary Magdalene, a woman described as "sinful" who is forgiven by Jesus in Luke 7, and Mary, the sister of Martha and Lazarus. This identification persisted for centuries in the Western Church, although the Eastern Orthodox Church never followed suit, keeping the women separate in its liturgical calendar and legends.

68. So, Gregory wanted to diminish Mary Magdalene's importance when he did this?

Not at all. If you actually read the homily in question, you'll see, first of all, that the conflation of these figures was an honest attempt to clear up some confusion and answer some questions. Secondly, Gregory didn't condemn Mary Magdalene at all! In fact, it was the opposite. Gregory held Mary Magdalene up as a model for all of his listeners: just as she let the loving forgiveness of Jesus into her life and was changed, so could they.

That's also the pattern for the way that Catholic devotion viewed Mary Magdalene in subsequent centuries as well. She was celebrated and held up as a model for both women and men, as one who had enjoyed the blessings of repentance and forgiveness — a sign, not of condemnation, but of hope.

FOR MORE INFORMATION...

To find out more about Mary Magdalene, see de-coding Mary Magdalene: Truth, Legend, and Lies (Our Sunday Visitor).

seven

WHO WAS LEONARDO?

69. According to *The Da Vinci Code*, who was Leonardo da Vinci?

The Da Vinci Code novel and movie present Leonardo, first of all, as a Grand Master of the Priory of Sion. Since the Priory of Sion was a group started in 1956 by an off-kilter Frenchman with a penchant for conspiracy, that's obviously impossible.

That alone should be enough to put *The Da Vinci Code* in its place. The Leonardo material is taken from *The Templar Revelation*, a book we mentioned in the first chapter, whose authors have also written books on UFOs.

We cannot state this strongly enough: *Art historians are universally aghast at the impact* The Da Vinci Code *has had on readers' views of Leonardo in particular and art in general.* In this work, Leonardo is misconstrued and caricatured, and the whole delicate, fascinating, subtle work of art interpretation and appreciation is stripped down to looking for hidden "codes" in a piece.

It would seem as if no more needed to be said. But for some, the *fact* that the Priory of Sion did not exist; the *logical conclusion* that, therefore, the assertions about Leonardo are false; and the *consistent testimony* of art historians to the falsity of *The Da Vinci Code*'s statements about art are, amazingly, not enough. They still "believe." They still insist that the figure to Jesus' right *must be* Mary Magdalene. Why? Because they read it in *The Da Vinci Code*.

70. What else does *The Da Vinci Code* get wrong about Leonardo?

First, it gets his name wrong. Dan Brown insists that he was inspired to write this novel, in part, by his wife, who, he says, is an art historian. He peoples his novel with "experts" discussing the life and work of Leonardo. The trouble is, all of them refer to the artist as "Da Vinci." That, of course, is not his name, but rather the place in which he was from — Vinci, a small town in Tuscany.

It seems like a small point, but it isn't. Someone who professes to be telling you the "real truth" about a subject would rightfully be expected to get something as basic as that person's name correct. If you look in an index to an art book, or in an encyclopedia for an entry on this artist, it would not be under "d" or "V," but under "L" — and the writer would *never* refer to him as "Da Vinci" but as "Leonardo."

Brown also mischaracterizes Leonardo's life and career. He says that he was a "flamboyant homosexual," when in fact hardly anything of Leonardo's romantic life is known at all. In 1476, as a young man, he (along with four others) was anonymously accused of a homosexual liaison. They were all acquitted. That incident does not make a "flamboyant homosexual."

Brown characterizes Leonardo as a painter, primarily of religious subjects. He writes that Leonardo had an "enormous output of breathtaking Christian art" and "hundreds" of Vatican commissions (*The Da Vinci Code*, p. 45). That's very, very wrong.

Leonardo, to begin with, was *not* primarily a painter at all. Yes, he did paint, but the bulk of his work involved drawings and scientific studies. He had a few religious subjects, and exactly one commission from a pope: Leo X. He spent most of that time conducting scientific experiments.

71. What about Leonardo's religious faith? *The Da Vinci Code* says that he was a devout nature worshiper, and that he was considered to be in a "perpetual state of sin" by the Church.

This is another misreading of history. After all, if Leonardo was such a pariah to the Church, why would the Vatican have given him the "hundreds" of commissions *The Da Vinci Code* says it did (which it didn't), or even the one he actually received?

Leonardo, of course, left voluminous journals behind, written in that backward script. Through reading those, we can have some sense of his religious beliefs.

Leonardo's writings certainly don't indicate what we might think of as traditional Christian beliefs, fully in tune with the teachings of the Catholic Church. But on the other hand, do remember that this *was* the Renaissance. It was a period of tremendous intellectual ferment, as Europeans rediscovered the forms and paradigms of ancient Greek and Roman art and thinking. There was great interest in the natural world and a growing engagement by artists with that natural world, as they worked to accurately represent it.

It's a mistake, however, to think that this activity stood in opposition to the Catholic Church. It didn't. The Church was actually the prime locus of intellectual activity during this period, and many of those who were deeply immersed in this engagement — even with the inheritance of pagan, classical culture — were clerics.

Leonardo definitely believed in God. Through his science and his art, he seemed to have primarily sought God through studying and re-presenting what God had created. He was not a practicing worshiper and, like many of his day, was deeply anti-clerical.

But Leonardo was not a "nature worshiper," devout or not, and was not thought ill of by Church leaders who, in fact, commissioned his work.

72. ***The Da Vinci Code* claims that Leonardo named the *Mona Lisa* as a way to communicate his commitment to the androgynous ideals of the real Jesus, by making anagrams of the names of an Egyptian god and goddess.**

There was no Priory of Sion, and no sense in the Renaissance that Jesus' teaching was about the "sacred feminine." Therefore, it's not possible.

If you need more, consider this: *Leonardo did not name this painting.* He didn't even mention it in his voluminous journals. It was not called "Mona Lisa" until years later, by a biographer of Leonardo.

73. What about *The Last Supper*?

Yes, what about it? There's much that Brown gets wrong about this painting, and we'll go into detail on that. But first, at the risk of being tedious, please remember this: Brown claims that Leonardo hid "codes" about the "real" relationship of Jesus and Mary Magdalene in this painting, because he was part of the Priory of Sion, which was guarding this secret. *There was no Priory of Sion. Therefore, this can't be true.* (Not to mention, once again, that Mary Magdalene plays no role in any Grail lore from the Middle Ages through the Renaissance, Leonardo's era.)

But, once more, because this kind of simple logic doesn't work for everyone, we'll get a little bit more specific. We'll focus on the depiction of this disputed figure.

74. Do you mean the figure called "John," but who is actually Mary Magdalene?

Yes, that one — although it is, indeed, John.

Brown's interpretation rests on the fact that this figure is beardless and, to some eyes, "feminine looking." Therefore it must really be a woman.

This assertion displays an impressive lack of understanding of art. During this period, the apostle John was almost always portrayed in this way — as quite youthful, beardless, and attractive. He is portrayed according to a "type" — the "Student." To say that the depiction of John in *The Last Supper* indicates that Leonardo was trying to depict Mary Magdalene would necessitate believing that every other Renaissance artist was trying to do the same thing.

There is much more that's wrong with Brown's interpretation, but we'd hope that this would be all that's necessary to make clear what reality — rather than fantasy — says about this work.

75. What about the other works?

Brown gets almost all of that wrong, too. Most notably, and humorously, is his description of the version of Leonardo's *Madonna of the Rocks* that is in the Louvre. His description of the painting's content is wrong, but what's even more ridiculous is his description of what Sophie Neveau does with the painting.

In her escape from the Louvre at the beginning of the novel, Sophie uses *The Madonna of the Rocks* as a shield and threatens to damage it. The novel describes her holding the painting up and bending the canvas with her knee.

The Madonna of the Rocks is six and a half feet high, and it is encased in a very heavy wooden frame. Once again, *The Da Vinci Code* gets it wrong — the scenario it describes is, frankly speaking, impossible.

76. So why does this matter?

It matters because it's one more example of the errors riddling this work. There's no "could be" about any of it. Brown gets his art wrong, and he gets his history wrong as well. As an art history professor said once in this writer's hearing, "People tell me how much they've learned about art from *The Da Vinci Code*. I just tell them they've learned *nothing* about art from *The Da Vinci Code!*"

FOR MORE INFORMATION . . .

To learn more about what **The Da Vinci Code** *gets wrong about Leonardo, see Chapter Eight of* **de-coding Da Vinci: The Facts Behind the Fiction of 'The Da Vinci Code'** *(Our Sunday Visitor).*

eight

THE CATHOLIC CHURCH: FACT AND FICTION

77. What does *The Da Vinci Code* say about the Catholic Church?

It tries to have it both ways. In the novel, the Church is constantly excoriated for oppressing women and suppressing truth. But there are a few offhanded positive remarks about the Church's charitable work, and in the end, the "real" bad guy in the story is revealed to be Teabing, the "Teacher," and not the Church.

But the overall effect is quite negative, an impression that is carried through to the movie, because the final conclusion the reader or viewer is urged to make is essentially that *the Catholic Church is the enemy of truth.*

78. How so?

Because of everything that we've discussed so far in this book: *The Da Vinci Code* maintains that the Jesus found in the Gospels is not the "real" Jesus. That "real" Jesus is to be found in Gnostic writings.

Therefore, *Da Vinci Code* logic tells us, the Church is responsible for suppressing truth.

79. What's wrong with that view?

It assumes that there was no logical reason to privilege the Gospels and the apostolic witness to Jesus' life and ministry they contain. It assumes that this tradition was "picked" because it served a political purpose.

And as we've seen, that's simply not supportable, and it's illogical.

80. Why is it illogical?

Because if it was all about picking stories that gave you the most political clout, the early Christian leaders did a lousy job, since they picked the story that got them excommunicated from their Jewish communities and then persecuted by the Roman Empire.

If the *Da Vinci Code* scenario about Mary Magdalene had been true, *that* story would have caused *no problems* for early Christians. There were many movements centered around wisdom teachers in the Roman Empire, and none of them were persecuted. Women were involved in various religious and spiritual traditions. There was no scandal there.

But that's not what happened. The Christian story, from its earliest appearance, holds to a consistent theme: that through Jesus, God had entered the world in a new, radical way. This man was executed as a criminal, but he rose from the dead. There is one God, and no one else — not any earthly emperor — may be honored as divine.

Sticking to this "story" got them persecuted, arrested, and executed themselves. This is very odd behavior for people seeking political power.

81. But the Church rejected the Gnostic writings, correct? Isn't that repression?

No. It's a rejection of falsehood.

The early centuries of Christian history were filled with intense theological discussion. For example, as we can see from a reading of the New Testament, the earliest Christians believed that Jesus was "Lord" and worshiped him, but what that meant in precise theological or philosophical terms was, not surprisingly, unclear. What does it *mean* to say that Jesus is Lord? There is but one God — how can we explain, then, the clear sense that the Father, the Son, and the Holy Spirit are all divine?

Add to that the fact that Christianity grew out of a Jewish context. When it came into contact with pagan philosophies and worldviews, work had to be done so that the truth the apostles had discerned about Jesus made sense to these new listeners.

Finally, with such a mysterious reality, there are bound to be diverse alternative explanations, and such was the case in these early centuries. For example, some thinkers decided that Jesus was fully divine, but not fully human, and that his body was a phantasm of sorts (Docetism). Other movements taught that Jesus wasn't fully divine, but rather a demigod of sorts (Arianism). Or some believed that he had been "adopted" by God as his Son at a crucial moment — at his baptism in the Jordan, for instance (Adoptionism).

82. Well, there were different opinions. What was wrong with that? Why did the Church care?

Because truth matters.

In reflecting on all of those different systems (heresies), Christian thinkers and teachers discerned that in every one of them, something was missing. Using what had been handed down by the apostolic witnesses to the life and ministry of Jesus, which we read in the Gospels and see reflected in other early writings, they saw that each of those "alternatives" was flawed in some way. In emphasizing one truth — for example, that Jesus was fully divine — they lost another, equally important truth — in this case, Jesus' inarguable humanity.

So, as those heresies emerged, Christians had to deal with them. And those ideas that were found to be deficient — that is, not embodying the whole truth of who Jesus was — were rejected and, yes, condemned.

Why? Because if people were to follow those ideas, they would be walking away from the truth about Jesus — as mysterious and tension-filled as it can be sometimes — that was handed down by those who were actual witnesses to his life and ministry.

That's not repressing truth. That's called *protecting truth.*

83. What about all those witches? *The Da Vinci Code* **says that the Catholic Church killed five million of them during the Middle Ages.**

It certainly does, and it further says that those five million women were not witches, but scholars, gypsies, mystics, nature lovers, and even midwives.

Five million. *That's a lot of people.*

84. But is it true? Is that what happened?

No. You might want to know, first of all, that this is not an issue that is ignored by historians. There's a great deal of actual research out there dealing with the question, and what follows is the general conclusion.

Between the years 1500 and 1800 (a period well past the Middle Ages), there were approximately forty thousand executions for witchcraft that took place in Europe and North America. Twenty percent of those executed were men. Some of the accused were tried by Catholic bodies, others by Protestants, and most by governments.

One scholar has done extensive research on a single period — the years between 1550 and 1630 — in France, Switzerland, and Germany, countries that were deep in post-Reformation turmoil and tension.

Most women condemned as witches were poor and disliked, and had been denounced, not by religious authorities, but by their neighbors. More than half of those accused were acquitted, and research shows that none of those who were eventually executed had been charged with practicing woman-centered pagan religion.

Those executions are, of course, reflective of a completely different mind-set, and are tragic and unjust. But it's still worth noting that the claim that "five million" women were executed as witches by the Catholic Church is a total fabrication.

85. What else does *The Da Vinci Code* **get wrong in its discussion of the Catholic Church?**

There's a great deal of discussion of the origins of Christian sacraments and iconography that's in the novel, all of which is incorrect. Most of this has not been transferred to the movie, so we won't discuss it here.

However, what does remain consistent in the movie is this odd characterization of the past and present that is almost a backhanded compliment to Catholicism.

Throughout *The Da Vinci Code*, the "Catholic Church" is presented as the locus of all of this Jesus-related thinking and teaching. The belief in Jesus' divinity is presented as a particular flaw of the Catholic Church.

That's strange because, of course, it's not only Catholics who believe that Jesus is divine. The Eastern Orthodox and Protestant Christians are on that train as well. It's not just the Catholic Church that accepts the four Gospels in the New Testament as authoritative. *All* Christians do.

Further, as we've seen, Protestants did plenty of heresy-hunting and witch-burning in their day. Catholic bishops were not in charge in seventeenth-century Salem, Massachusetts.

However, for some odd reason, despite the shared beliefs of Christians, it is not "Christianity" that *The Da Vinci Code* identifies as the culprit, the enemy of Jesus' "true" intentions, but only the Catholic Church.

In one way, it's a compliment, in that *The Da Vinci Code* evidently sees the Catholic Church as the primary locus of Christianity.

But in another way, it's not. It's simple, ignorant, and malicious anti-Catholicism, the likes of which we've seen before, and will doubtless see again.

FOR MORE INFORMATION...

To learn more about the issues discussed in this chapter, see Chapters Seven and Ten of de-coding Da Vinci: The Facts Behind the Fiction of 'The Da Vinci Code' (Our Sunday Visitor).

nine

SWEATING THE SMALL STUFF

86. What about women? *The Da Vinci Code* **suggests that until Christianity came, women were worshiped and revered. Christianity introduced patriarchy and women's lot changed forever.**

There is a *great deal* of mythmaking in that scenario. It's a rather stunning oversimplification of historical reality.

But it's also not uncommon. What *The Da Vinci Code* picks up on is the idea — promoted through some pop history and spirituality over the past four decades especially — that in ancient times the "sacred feminine" was widely revered, and that woman's mysterious relationship with nature was the power center of spirituality.

87. It wasn't?

It doesn't seem to be. In the late nineteenth century, some researchers hypothesized and promoted an ancient era of reverencing a "Mother Goddess," in which women were seen as not only equal to males, but also, at some level, reverenced in a unique way. The conclusions were rooted in interpretations of archaeological finds like pregnant female figures and cave openings interpreted by some to be womb-like. It was said by some that this era was supplanted by Indo-Europeans who swept across the land and replaced the Mother Goddess with the warrior god and patriarchy.

In recent years, the ambiguous nature of these artifacts, the discovery of — yes — weapons, and strong indications of traditional gender-based division of labor in many of these same sites (which were used to build up the Mother Goddess hypothesis) have led to the conclusion that there is, in the end, no evidence to suggest that such an era ever existed.

88. But what about the worship of both gods and goddesses? *The Da Vinci Code* makes a big deal of this.

Yes, it does. Dan Brown has asserted that he's glad to bring this "hidden history" of the past worship of gods and goddesses into the light.

The trouble is, it's not hidden, and it doesn't mean what he says it does.

Certainly, pagan religions have both male and female deities that are worshiped. Some of them — very few — have even included fertility rituals. Brown, however, draws the conclusion that because of this, those societies were egalitarian (an egalitarianism that was destroyed by patriarchy), and that the fertility rituals were about the reunion of the male and female principles in reality.

He's wrong on both counts. First of all, one need only consider ancient Greek, Roman, African, or Asian cultures that involved goddess worship. Were these egalitarian societies? Of course not, and the irony is that it is *Christianity* that historically has been responsible for elevating the status of women in these cultures.

Secondly, fertility rites, for the most part, served a more mundane purpose than spiritual androgyny: fertility of crops, livestock, and human beings, as the name indicates.

89. But the Catholic Church *has* repressed women's spirituality, hasn't it?

Let's be realistic here. We already discussed how popular a saint Mary Magdalene was. If you know even a little bit about Christian history, you know that there are many female saints, women who have been revered and honored by both men and women for their holiness and service to others.

And finally, we might want to consider one important figure that *The Da Vinci Code* studiously ignores: Mary, the mother of Jesus.

When you consider the Blessed Virgin Mary's importance in Catholic spirituality, and you then consider that some Christians in other denominations criticize Catholicism for putting *too much* emphasis on Mary, you see how far off *The Da Vinci Code* is on this score.

Of course, Brown ignores Mary and the profoundly feminine spirituality she has represented in Catholicism for hundreds of years. He has to do this, or else his argument, such as it is, collapses.

90. What about the Church of Saint-Sulpice? Is that real?

Yes, the Church of Saint-Sulpice actually does exist in Paris, and yes, there is the "Rose Line" spoken of in *The Da Vinci Code*. The problem is that, not surprisingly, the origins and function of the Rose Line are mischaracterized. The novel and the movie declare that the Rose Line — a thin brass strip embedded in the floor — is of pagan roots and points to the secrets of the Grail hidden within the church.

Of course, all of this is false — there are no Grail secrets hidden within the church, and the "P" and "S" on one of the stained glass windows refer, not to the Priory of Sion, but to Peter and Sulpitius (Sulpice), the two patron saints of the church.

The Da Vinci Code suggests that the line has some sort of pagan implications. The sister who is the caretaker of the church describes it as a "gnomon . . . a pagan astronomical device."

That's like describing the Pythagorean theorem as a pagan idea. There are innumerable notions, concepts, and tools that have emerged from "pagan" cultures, but that doesn't mean that their use implies devotion to pagan religions. But that's the implication of this statement.

No, the fact is something that's actually far more interesting: the "Rose Line," gnomon, or as it was more commonly called, *meridiana*, was a part of many large Catholic churches during the seventeenth and eighteenth centuries. Why? Because in those days when interest in science was growing, but before the development of large telescopes that could take accurate and consistent measurements, it was discovered that churches could actually be very useful in that regard.

How? By placing a line in a certain position on the floor, and then making a hole in the roof, the movements of the earth around the sun could be followed, as a single sharp ray of sunlight pierced through the hole and, as the year progressed, followed a path along the floor. The ray of sunlight would touch certain points at solstices and equinoxes, allowing observers not only to expand their understanding of the earth and sun's relationship, but to accurately determine the date of Easter.

These churches — which include not only Saint-Sulpice but also Santa Maria degli Angeli in Rome, in which a *meridiana* was constructed at the order of none other than the pope — were, in essence, the first solar observatories. Not bad for a Church "dedicated" to discouraging the pursuit of knowledge and truth.

Perhaps the final word on this should go to the *real* caretakers of Saint-Sulpice themselves, who have erected a sign in response to the deluge of *Da Vinci Code* visitors:

> Contrary to fanciful allegations in a recent best-selling novel, this is not a vestige of a pagan temple. No such temple ever existed in this place. It was never called a "Rose Line." It does not coincide with the meridian traced through the middle of the Paris Observatory, which serves as a reference for maps where longitudes are measured in degrees East or West of Paris. No mystical notion can be derived from this.

91. And the Knights Templar?

Yes, they're in *The Da Vinci Code* as well. They're described as the military arm of the Priory of Sion, which was mercilessly destroyed by Pope Clement V.

There's about 2 percent fact in that story and the rest is just wrong.

The Knights Templar were, indeed, a military group — one of a few "military orders" formed during the Middle Ages. Their members took vows, including one of poverty, followed a particular spiritual regime, and were committed to a particular task.

In this case, the Knights Templar began, in the twelfth century, as a small group organized to protect Christian pilgrims to Jerusalem against harassment and attack from Muslims. It soon evolved into a relatively small but effective group of warriors who fought in the Crusades.

The knights also established a banking system, the fruit of the vow of poverty. New members would donate their goods and wealth to the order. The holdings then enabled them to loan money, first to pilgrims traveling to the Holy Land, and eventually to others as well.

The decline of the Knights Templar is rooted in their involvement in banking, and was hastened, not by the pope, but by the French king Philip the Fair. The situation was complicated, but in essence, Philip was determined to strip the knights of their wealth and power. It was he, not the pope, who ordered the arrests and eventual executions.

In addition, Pope Clement V actually did call for an investigation of the Knights Templar, which found little to no heresy. In 1312, the pope did suppress the knights and order them to disperse their holdings, but he took those actions because of the scandal and damage done to the order by Philip the Fair's war against it. The "massacre" on Friday the 13th, 1307, is another distortion. On that day, members of the Knights Templar across France *were* arrested, but by the French king, not by the pope. There was no massacre, but there were subsequent trials in which the knights were charged with crimes that, ironically, Philip had issued against Pope Boniface VIII in his power struggle with the pontiff.

Not exactly the simple scenario proposed in *The Da Vinci Code*. But by now, that shouldn't surprise you a bit.

FOR MORE INFORMATION...

To learn more about the issues discussed in this chapter, see Chapters Six and Nine of de-coding Da Vinci: The Facts Behind the Fiction of 'The Da Vinci Code' (Our Sunday Visitor).

ten

'ALL HISTORY IS FICTION'

92. All of this seems to come down to how you view history, doesn't it?

It certainly does. Very early in *The Da Vinci Code* movie, the Robert Langdon character intones that *all history is fiction*. This is a constant running theme through the novel and the movie, and it is taken in a couple of directions:

- That we can never say what *really* happened in the past because everything is experienced through the prism of personal interpretation.
- That the events of the past are recorded by the "winners" who have a political stake in promoting their version of events. Therefore, the equally valid version experienced by the "losers" is lost.

In his promotion of the novel, Dan Brown said this explicitly:

> Since the beginning of recorded time, history has been written by the "winners" (those societies and belief systems that conquered and survived). Despite an obvious bias in this accounting method, we still measure the "historical accuracy" of a given concept by examining how well it concurs with our existing historical record. Many historians now believe (as do I) that in gauging the historical accuracy of a given concept, we should first ask ourselves a far deeper question: How historically accurate is history itself? (www.danbrown.com/novels/davinci_code/faqs.html)

93. Isn't that true?

As is so often the case with *The Da Vinci Code*, the answer is yes *and* no.

Historians must, of course, take into account all sorts of sources from all sides in reconstructing the events of the past. Historical interpretations shift as we learn more — say, for example, about the precise causes of the fall of the Roman Empire or the origins of the American Civil War.

But those kinds of disputes and arguments — about *why* something happened — are not what Brown is talking about. He's suggesting that *what* we read about should be naturally suspect.

Well, in a way it should, because there is, indeed, much ambiguity about the past, and there are always new things to be learned.

But what Brown is implying is that the basic story of the origins of Christianity is in dispute because its history has been written by "winners" — one can presume the "Peter party," of whom he writes so often, the side determined to undermine Mary Magdalene. His whole story is based on this premise: that the Church has suppressed the truth about early Christianity.

In fact, the conclusion of both *The Da Vinci Code* novel and movie points back to the first level of questioning we raised: You've almost got a sense of hands being thrown up in the air and a "whatever" resonating through the universe. Hey, Mary Magdalene *could have been* a spouse and goddess ... or not.

This questioning comes up quite a bit in discussions of *The Da Vinci Code*, which is why it's important to have them. People say, "We can't know what *really* happened. It was too long ago. The sources are too scarce. Different people interpret events in different ways. History is written by the winners. So who knows?"

Now let's think about what the ultimate conclusion is, then: *That the past is totally unknowable, and anything could be true. Or nothing. Whatever version you pick is okay.*

That's just absurd.

94. But there *is* an element of interpretation in history, isn't there?

Of course. And certainly it is sometimes difficult to discern the reality of what happened. But that doesn't mean *anything can be correct*. And *that's* the final conclusion of *The Da Vinci Code*: All history is fiction.

Let's look at early Christianity, since that's the topic at hand. Is it really true that the whole era is a total mystery, and that no one can ever know what Jesus really did and said?

Of course not. And we've seen in the fourth chapter that the accounts of Jesus' ministry — what he said and did — are consistent in those early sources, written down just decades after the events they describe.

The bottom line is this, and it is quite important: Historians do, indeed, interpret Jesus' life and ministry in different ways. There are disputes and disagreements about countless issues: What was Jesus' relationship to establishment Judaism of his day? What exactly were his hopes and intentions for the movement he was starting, and did he even intend to start a movement at all? What was this "kingdom of God" that Jesus preached about?

But *The Da Vinci Code* notions that Jesus' ministry was essentially about the reunion of male and female principles in reality, and that Mary Magdalene was his wife and chosen successor — sorry, folks, but these are not among the disputed points. They are *fiction — all made up by twentieth-century conspiracist pseudo-historians.*

So there's no "could have" about it.

95. What about the "history written by the winners"? Couldn't the Catholic "winners" simply have repressed the truth?

Here's the thing: There is no great mystery about what alternative interpretations of Jesus early Christians ran up against. Many of their critical writings have survived. We covered the disputes in our chapter on Gnosticism (Chapter Four: Early Christian History) — they were mostly about theological interpretations of Jesus' nature and the definition of the Trinity during those early centuries, most of them turning on rather fine philosophical points.

The point is that we have a fairly good understanding of the dynamic of development of early Christian thinking — what they believed and what heresies they responded to. Do an Internet search for "Early Christian Fathers" or "Patristics" and you will get an excellent sense of this. Nowhere in there, not even in the disputes with the Gnostics, is there any hint of the kind of conflict Brown — and the works he bases his book on — describes.

It just didn't happen.

96. You can't prove Jesus' divinity from this, you know.

I'm not trying to, even though a lot of people make the quite illogical jump from trying to clarify what early Christians believed about Jesus to what you, right now, should believe about Jesus.

Showing that the most reliable witnesses to the ministry and life of Jesus viewed him as "Lord" and worshiped him is just describing a historical reality. It doesn't "prove" that he is divine — that is, indeed, a decision we make, based on evidence, ourselves.

97. I'm still skeptical.

Well, that's not a bad thing. The only thing you should be wary of is this: Are you an equal-opportunity skeptic? Or do you bring *more* skepticism to the discussion of Christian history than you do, say, Roman history of the same period?

If so, you might want to ask yourself why.

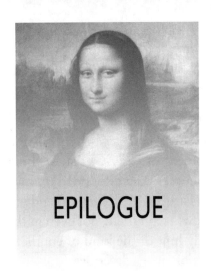

EPILOGUE

As I travel around the country speaking on *The Da Vinci Code*, the same questions seem to pop up over and over. Many of them have been addressed in this book. But there are three more general queries that merit a final, brief chapter of their own.

98. Should I read the book or see the movie *The Da Vinci Code*? Everyone's talking about it, and I need to be able to discuss it.

That's up to you. I'd be concerned with two consequences:

- Wasting some of the already brief time I've got to spend on this earth on drivel.
- Lining the pockets of those who have perpetuated such an intellectual travesty.

And frankly, contrary to what some might try to get you to believe, it's not necessary to read the book or see the movie in order to engage the issues.

The issues are straightforward and can be easily listed – just go through the table of contents at the front of this book. There's nothing about the plot, the writing, the acting, or the cinematography of these works that enhances one's understanding of these points. They don't emerge out of subtle writing or directing. They're offered by characters in speeches that they make to one another, before they go off to the next part of the chase.

Books like *de-coding Da Vinci* provide a plot synopsis, and this booklet and that book provide an adequate debunking.

By all means, engage in the dialogue about this movie. It's an important opportunity to explore the truths about early Christian history. Don't be afraid at all of that dialogue. But as for the book or movie? As I said: Life is short.

99. I like fiction. I'm intrigued by fiction that has spiritual or religious themes. Is there anything out there besides *The Da Vinci Code* that I could read?

Certainly there is. And to be honest, we'd all be much better off if we took even half as much time as has been spent on *The Da Vinci Code* and applied it instead to reading and "dialoguing" about some of these other works that I'm about to mention. These writers grapple with *real* faith issues, not titillating, empty pseudo-history:

- Fyodor Dostoevsky: *The Brothers Karamazov; Crime and Punishment; The Idiot*
- Graham Greene: *The Power and the Glory; The End of the Affair; The Heart of the Matter*
- Evelyn Waugh: *Brideshead Revisited; Helena*
- Flannery O'Connor: *Wise Blood; Collected Stories; The Habit of Being*
- Walker Percy: *The Moviegoer; Love in the Ruins; The Thanatos Syndrome*
- Muriel Spark: *Momento Mori*
- Brian Moore: *Catholics; Black Robe*
- François Mauriac: *Vipers' Tangle; A Woman of the Pharisees*
- George Bernanos: *Diary of a Country Priest*
- Edwin O'Connor: *The Edge of Sadness*
- J.F. Powers: *Morte D'Urban*
- Jon Hassler: *North of Hope; A Green Journey*
- Rumer Godden: *In This House of Brede*
- Myles Connolly: *Mr. Blue*
- Ron Hansen: *Mariette in Ecstasy; Atticus*

If you're interested in the intersection of faith and movie, you might try these:

- *The Passion of Joan of Arc* (1928)
- *The Mission (1986)*
- *Thérèse (1986)*
- *Babette's Feast (1987)*
- *A Man for All Seasons (1966)*
- *The Decalogue (1988)*
- *On the Waterfront (1954)*
- *The Apostle (1998)*

These are just some personal favorites, and there are many more. Questions of faith are so elemental to human life that they have provided powerful themes for countless serious writers and filmmakers.

100. What's the worst mistake in *The Da Vinci Code?*

There are so many, it's impossible to pick just one! The list of what this book gets right would be far shorter than what it gets wrong.

However, there is one point that is probably the "most" wrong, an assumption that undergirds the entire work, and which might actually do some damage. It's this: *Throughout the novel and the movie, the claim is made that the Gnostic writings presented a more "human Jesus," and that this "human Jesus" was a figure that the Church was determined to repress in favor of its All-Divine-All-The-Time model, which supposedly cemented the institution's power.*

So, the Jesus of the Gnostic writings is *more* human than the Jesus of the Gospels and the Church?

Really?

If you believe that, then you've never read a Gospel.

If you believe that, then you've never set foot in a Catholic church.

Why? Because, as we learned earlier, when you read the Gnostic writings, you meet the most unearthly, abstract — and frankly speaking — boring, barely human figure you can imagine. He walks around talking, talking, and talking. He doesn't suffer, and for sure he doesn't die.

But when you actually sit down and read a Gospel, what do you see? Or rather, *whom* do you see?

You meet a man who was born of a woman, who, it is said in the Gospel of Luke, "increased in wisdom" (2:52). He eats with his friends, goes visiting, gets into arguments, has to get away from people at times, weeps, and is even afraid. He dies. On a cross, in agony, he dies.

You're going to tell me *that's* not human?

Think about Christian iconography as well. What are the two most frequent ways of depicting Jesus that you see in two thousand years of devotional art, from a Church that's "intent" on suppressing the humanity of Jesus? An infant on his mother's lap, and a man suffering his death throes.

You're going to tell me *that's* not human?

So yes, those who are enraptured and obsessed with *The Da Vinci Code*, who believe its lies, are being misled. For the truth is exactly the reverse of what this work would have you believe: It's the *Christian Church* that has preserved, in that mysterious but necessary tension, the full humanity of the One it also proclaims as Lord.

I sometimes wonder why people are so fascinated with the Jesus of *The Da Vinci Code* and why they so resolutely ignore the Jesus we meet in the Gospels and meet through the Church; why people don't want to take that Jesus seriously; why they just want to brush him off and focus on esoteric, abstract, windy speeches on inner light offered by a stick figure.

But then I go back to the Gospels, and I read: *Sell everything you have and give the money to the poor. . . . Love your enemies. . . . Feed the hungry. . . . Clothe the naked. . . . Visit the imprisoned. . . . Blessed are the poor. . . . Blessed are those who mourn. . . . Blessed are the peacemakers. . . . What you do to the least of these, you do to me. . . . The last shall be first. . . .*

Of course. No surprise. No wonder we don't want *him* to be the real Jesus. No surprise at all.